TARANTULA VS. PIRANHA

Gareth Stevens
PUBLISHING

By Jill Keppeler

Please visit our website, www.garethstevens.com. For a free color catalog of all our high-quality books, call toll free 1-800-542-2595 or fax 1-877-542-2596.

Library of Congress Cataloging-in-Publication Data

Names: Keppeler, Jill, author.
Title: Tarantula vs. piranha / Jill Keppeler.
Description: New York : Gareth Stevens Publishing, [2019] | Series: Bizarre
    beast battles | Includes index.
Identifiers: LCCN 2018003834| ISBN 9781538219393 (library bound) | ISBN
    9781538219416 (paperback) | ISBN 9781538219423 (6 pack)
Subjects: LCSH: Tarantulas–Juvenile literature. | Piranhas–Juvenile
    literature. | Animal behavior–Juvenile literature. | Animal
    weapons–Juvenile literature. | Adaptation (Biology)–Juvenile literature.
Classification: LCC QL458.42.T5 K47 2019 | DDC 595.4/4–dc23
LC record available at https://lccn.loc.gov/2018003834

First Edition

Published in 2019 by
Gareth Stevens Publishing
111 East 14th Street, Suite 349
New York, NY 10003

Copyright © 2019 Gareth Stevens Publishing

Designer: Katelyn E. Reynolds
Editor: Monika Davies

Photo credits: Cover, p. 1 (tarantula) Dr Bill Dixon/Shutterstock.com; cover, p. 1 (piranha) hasky2/Shutterstock.com; cover, pp. 1–24 (background texture) Apostrophe/Shutterstock.com; pp. 4–21 (tarantula icon) Kazakov Maksim/ Shutterstock.com; pp. 4–21 (piranha icon) Ziablik/Shutterstock.com; p. 5 Audrey Snider-Bell/Shutterstock.com; p. 7 guentermanaus/Shutterstock.com; pp. 8, 16 reptiles4all/Shutterstock.com; p. 9 Julian Popov/Shutterstock.com; p. 10 asawinimages/Shutterstock.com; p. 11 marktucan/Shutterstock.com; p. 12 Ryan M. Bolton/Shutterstock.com; p. 13 John Madere/Corbis/Getty Images; p. 14 Anton Eine/EyeEm/Getty Images; p. 15 Vladimir Wrangel/Shutterstock.com; p. 17 Tom Brakefield/Stockbyte/Getty Images; p. 18 Marysha/Shutterstock.com; p. 19 Hayati Kayhan/Shutterstock.com; p. 21 (tarantula) Tim Flach/Stone/Getty Images; p. 21 (piranha) DOELAN Yann/hemis.fr/Getty Images.

Printed in the United States of America

CPSIA compliance information: Batch #CS18GS: For further information contact Gareth Stevens, New York, New York at 1-800-542-2595.

CONTENTS

Words in the glossary appear in **bold** type the first time they are used in the text.

TERRIFYING TARANTULAS

Spiders—especially tarantulas—frighten a lot of people! These large, hairy spiders live all over the world, mostly in warmer areas. There are about 900 species, or kinds, of tarantulas that we know of.

Tarantulas are carnivorous, or meat-eating, spiders that live in a few different **habitats**, though most live in rain forests. All of them have **fangs** which release venom, or poison, that they use to kill their **prey**. Sometimes, though, these big spiders will bite other animals—including humans!

LIKE MOST SPIDERS, TARANTULAS HAVE EIGHT LEGS AND EIGHT EYES.

POINTY-TOOTHED PIRANHAS

It might seem strange to be scared of a small fish, but piranhas pack quite a bite! These sharp-toothed fish live in freshwater, such as rivers and lakes, in South America. There are more than 60 species of piranhas, and 20 of these species can be found in the Amazon River.

Many horror movies have been made starring piranhas. These movies often show piranhas eating humans who have fallen into their watery home. But do piranhas really live up to their deadly **reputation**? Maybe not!

PIRANHAS CAN ALSO BE CALLED CARIBES. THESE FISH HAVE LIVED IN SOUTH AMERICA FOR MILLIONS OF YEARS!

SMALL BUT SCARY

One's a land animal and one's a fish, but what would happen if a tarantula fought a piranha? Let's see how they match up!

The largest tarantula is the goliath bird-eating tarantula of South America. This huge spider is about the size of a dinner plate!

 LEG SPAN OF A GOLIATH BIRD-EATING TARANTULA: up to 12 inches (30.5 cm)

 LENGTH OF A GOLIATH BIRD-EATING TARANTULA'S BODY: up to 4.75 inches (12 cm)

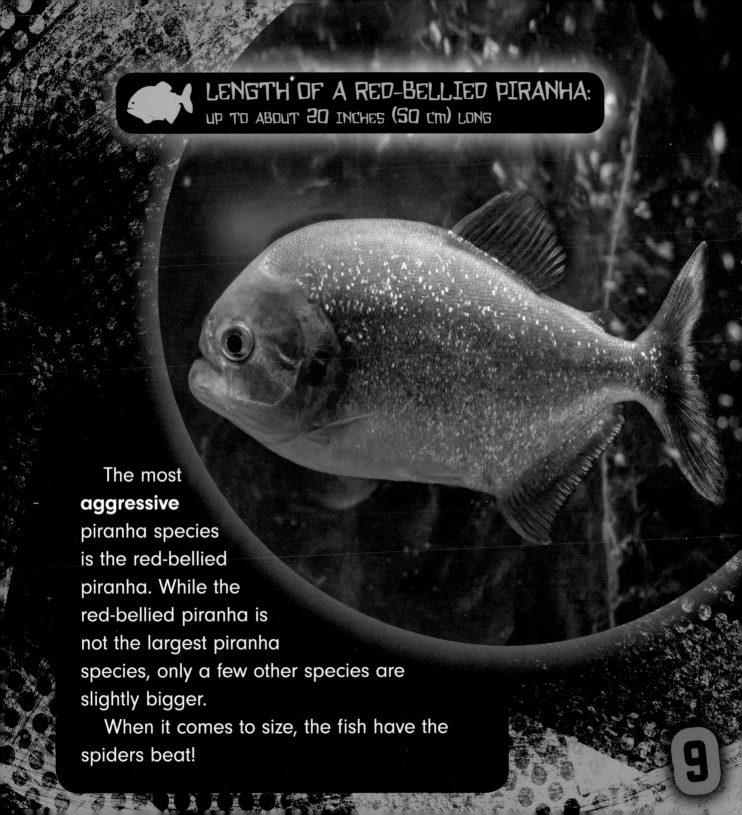

The most **aggressive** piranha species is the red-bellied piranha. While the red-bellied piranha is not the largest piranha species, only a few other species are slightly bigger.

When it comes to size, the fish have the spiders beat!

9

TOOTHY TROUBLE

Piranhas are known for their sharp teeth, and all tarantulas have fangs. Both sound frightening, but which animal has the more dangerous teeth?

Tarantula fangs are next to each other and point downward. Their fangs are sharp like needles!

LENGTH OF GOLIATH BIRD-EATING TARANTULA'S FANGS: 0.8 INCHES (2 cm)

Red-bellied piranhas have the sharpest teeth of any piranha species. Their triangular teeth snap together like scissor blades.

Tarantulas have longer fangs, but they only have two fangs each. Every piranha has two rows of very sharp teeth!

POISON AND POWER

There's more to the dangers of these animals than the size or number of their teeth. Both have bites that can hurt animals and humans in other ways.

Almost all tarantulas use their fangs to **inject** venom into their prey. However, tarantula venom rarely kills anything large.

TARANTULA VENOM:
- ABOUT AS STRONG AS BEE VENOM
- USUALLY NOT HARMFUL TO HUMANS

BLACK PIRANHA'S BITE FORCE:
- UP TO 72 POUNDS PER SQUARE INCH
- STRONGEST BITE FORCE RECORDED OF ANY BONY FISH

Piranhas don't have any venom, but they have a very powerful bite. A piranha's bite could take down a number of large animals given the chance! Piranhas rarely attack large animals, though.

SCARY SENSES

Tarantulas and piranhas both have senses that help them survive—and hunt other animals. Could a sneaky spider beat a hunting piranha?

Although tarantulas have eight eyes, these spiders can't see very well. They sense their prey through **vibrations**.

TARANTULA SENSES:

- POOR VISION, CAN ONLY SEE LIGHT, DARKNESS, AND MOVEMENT
- NO EARS
- USES BODY HAIRS TO FEEL VIBRATIONS

PIRANHA SENSES:

- EYES ON THE SIDES OF THEIR HEAD ALLOW THEM TO SEE FAR
- PAIRED NOSTRILS FOR SMELLING
- USES THEIR LATERAL LINE, OR A LINE OF SENSE ORGANS ALONG THEIR SIDE, TO FEEL VIBRATIONS OF OBJECTS OR PREY IN THE WATER

Piranhas have excellent hearing and a strong sense of smell. They can smell blood up to 2 miles (3.2 km) away!

15

OTHER DEFENSES

If piranhas and tarantulas couldn't use their teeth or fangs to chomp each other, could either of them win this beast battle? Do these animals have any other **defenses**?

A TARANTULA WILL HOLD UP ITS FRONT LEGS TO LOOK BIGGER WHEN FACING AN ENEMY.

A PIRANHA WILL MAKE A BARKING NOISE TO TELL OTHER FISH TO BACK OFF AND STAY AWAY.

Many kinds of tarantulas can defend themselves with their hairs! They **shed** hairs from their **abdomen** and flick them at enemies. These hairs can land in the eyes of their enemies, causing itching and pain.

A piranha's main means of defense is their teeth. A toothless piranha wouldn't have much defense against a tarantula at all!

17

WORKING TOGETHER

Neither tarantulas nor piranhas are very big, but do either of these creatures use teamwork to take down an enemy or prey?

Tarantulas tend to be **solitary** animals. They live alone and only meet up with other tarantulas when it is time to **mate**.

TARANTULAS ON THE HUNT:

- HUNT ALONE
- LOOK FOR PREY AT NIGHT
- MAINLY HUNT INSECTS
- MAY ALSO EAT SMALL SNAKES, LIZARDS, AND FROGS

PIRANHAS ON THE HUNT:

- FIRST ATTACK THE TAIL OR EYES OF THEIR PREY
- USUALLY HUNT FISH, INSECTS, SHRIMP, AND OTHER SMALL PREY
- RARELY ATTACK HUMANS
- OFTEN TRAVEL IN A SHOAL FOR PROTECTION, NOT TO HUNT PREY

Piranhas swim together in groups called shoals. A piranha that finds prey will **signal** others. A shoal of many piranhas can clear the meat off a large animal! Piranhas work well as a team.

19

THE WINNER?

Tarantulas look frightening. Their fangs are sharp and their bite can hurt, but this spider's venom isn't that strong. Piranhas have a greater number of sharp teeth, and a group of piranhas can work together to take down prey.

It's unlikely that a piranha and a tarantula would ever meet because one lives in water and one lives on land. They wouldn't survive in each other's habitats. But if they could meet, it would be quite a fight!

 NOW THAT YOU HAVE THE FACTS, WHO DO YOU THINK WOULD WIN THIS BEAST BATTLE?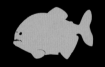

GLOSSARY

abdomen: the part of a creature's body that contains the stomach

aggressive: showing a readiness to attack

defense: a way of guarding against an enemy

fang: a long, pointed tooth

habitat: the natural place where an animal or plant lives

inject: to use sharp teeth to force venom into an animal's body

mate: to come together to make babies

prey: an animal that is hunted by other animals for food

reputation: the views that are held about something or someone

shed: to get rid of something

signal: to let someone know something using a sign or action

solitary: living, hunting, or working alone

vibration: a rapid movement back and forth

FOR MORE INFORMATION

BOOKS

Gish, Melissa. *Piranhas*. Mankato, MN: Creative Education, 2018.

Hely, Patrick. *Tarantulas*. New York, NY: PowerKids Press, 2018.

Pallotta, Jerry. *Tarantula vs. Scorpion: Who Would Win?* New York City, NY: Scholastic, 2016.

WEBSITES

Red-Bellied Piranha
kids.nationalgeographic.com/animals/red-bellied-piranha/#red-bellied-piranha-bellies.jpg
Learn more about the scariest piranhas with National Geographic.

Tarantula: Super Spiders
kids.sandiegozoo.org/animals/tarantula
Read fun facts about tarantulas, the "super spiders."

INDEX